Sweet kitty Chili Pepper

Stories

By C.P. Espien

Sweet kitty Chili Pepper

Sweet kitty Chili Pepper

ACKNOWLEDGEMENTS

These are real life, inspired stories.
Chili Pepper is our sweet cat and it has been
o joy ever since she joined our family.
Life is surprising!

I dedicate this book to my dear Catalin!

Sweet kitty Chili Pepper

Your dedication:

To ....

From: ....

Date: ....

CONTENTS

Sweet kitty Chili Pepper

Sweet kitty Chili Pepper

ACKNOWLEDGMENTS

This book is about telling in short stories, the amazing and unexpected experience of having a kitty, and how along with her, she brought into our life's, a new sense of kindness, joy, care, and many other, beautiful unfelt before emotions.

It is about how a small fur ball, managed to give us what we all people can give, and all want to receive, unconditional affection. And a million moment of surprisingly cuteness that melts our hearts.

She taught us peaceful relaxation and remembered us that naps, at any time of the day are part of a balanced and happy life.

She gave and still gives us countless precious moments.

All my love to you, sweet beige ball of fur, our dear Chili Pepper.

1 HOW ALL BEGAN

In one tiny cardboard box cover with the sweater I had on me, is staying quietly a small beige fur ball, with two sparkling eyes, scanning all around.

We are smiling to one another, happy that this small and sweet creature, who looked like a fury beautiful brooch, light weight as a feather, is finally coming home with us.

It didn't take long until she starts yelling and try to escape, but after talking with her for a few minutes, she sits cozy in one corner, slipping with her nose on her paws, just opening briefly the eyes from time to time, as the road directions is making her startle.

We arrived home!

I just took her out of the box right in the living room and let her easy on the carpet.

- You are home, go and discover all.

And that is what she did.

As the most natural thing, she starts to walk around, see, and smell everything, she finds the fire place and stays for a while in front of it, she comes to our feet, looks up, and then with a playful attitude, runs and starts playing with a stuffed squirrel that was on the floor, just waiting for her.

For the next days all is following its natural course, she follows us wherever we go, she is climbing in bed, even if I am trying to make her stay in the cozy place, I made for her on the couch.

Some other times she is going straight up on Cata's bely, and sleeps there, or up, face to face, and scares him, from his sleep.

The days start to look different with her in our life, being all that playful and quiet, always looking to be spoiled and loved, and giving in return one of the most beautiful feelings we have ever felt, these feelings of unconditional love, joy and affection.

It is as if each day we have something that wasn't here before her coming into our lives.

It brings us joy, and a sense of peaceful relaxation, when we are staying on TV and she is scouting the area, as if she is ignoring us, and then from the back of the couch she climbs up right between us, descend on Catalin's shoulder, where she stays for a while, following her trip to the small, almost un existing place between us.

Here is where she camps, for a few good hours.

And this is how the story begins.
Is truly one of those moments, when we are wondering:

- "How come, we didn't have a kitty, until now?!"

These stories are about how love entered into our live at another dimension then we already knew, and made us understand that there is much more to discover and enjoy in the same time.

2 THE STORY ABOUT GETTING HOME

One day she was in a pile of hay with all her other siblings, and after a long, noisy road, she got to a totally new place for her, that had no hay, but still much more other fluffy and cozy places, that on the way she will explore them one by one.

After getting her home, we went to take some stuff for her from the pet store.

She has now a box with some nice smelly stuff in it, that she really enjoys, and she even goes herself when she needs. Yeeii!

In a way she seems to know that this is making us happy, she appreciates that special place, and she goes every time just to the litter box.

She is such a smart and with good manners kitty! 😊

One thing is the same here, after day, night slowly comes too, and instead of going to her pile of hay, she looks like she is wondering:

- ''Where am I going to sleep?! Is that place of the couch where they putted
  me, intended to be my bed? But it is only a swatter! I need something puffier to dive

in for a good sleep.

Hm…let's see!

This people are nice, they feed me and played with me, gave me a place on the couch, but where are they going now?"

Following us with the corner of her eyes she saws us going in the most cozy and fluffy bed she ever believed to exist, and as we got off the light, she takes slowly her paws on a walk to see how is it to sleep in such a bed!

She is very smart, waiting for a while, hoping that we are asleep, and then she is sneaking near my legs, staying close, after a while she hides behind my back as if she wouldn't what me to know she is there, only feeling the warmth of her beige fury body.

She just takes one more glance, around!
- "Yes, it feels nice, this is home!"

Nighty night!

The most wonderful place in the world is the place we can call home, is that feeling of coziness that no matter where it is, we immediately know.

And all tucked in that fluffy and comfy pillow, near us, this sweet kitty, found her home!

3 THE STORY ABOUT THE ELEGANT DAY NAP

After a good night sleep, well hided in the fluffy bed, our dear kitty woke up, went straight to her little plate, with goodies, she eats her good juice breakfast, from one of those yummy one meal treats, drinks some water, and then as scouting the area, she comes and stays with us.

After a while she starts to clean herself, knowing exactly what she has to do, looking at us like she wanted to be seen, and appreciate, didn't miss one spot on her puffy beige fur, and after we saw a million contortionist positions used by her to clean, she decided that it's time for a nap.

She went straight to the sweater that we had put for her a night before. It seems that she likes it for the day nap.

We are impressed of this tiny ball of fur, not bigger than a palm, that has already figured things around her.

She looks again, at us, as if she was telling to herself:

- "After all this nice breakfast and a spa session, I well deserve a good day nap, with this

nice people watching over me!
    - I think I like them!"
    And then, taking the most elegant day sleep position, I have ever seen, she falls asleep.
    Looking at her we cannot believe our eyes, what a delicate and sweet little soul this kitty can be, taking her nap, one of many to come, and has such a natural way of doing everything as if she knew already everything.

Nice place!

4 THE STORY ABOUT THE YARD

As we were minding our own businesses, with something to do in the back yard, all of a sudden, we saw that the little cutie is standing near us, not making a sound just looking and taking all in, as if she is doing breading exercises.

It looks like, that after a well-deserved nap, she got up and not seeing us in site, she walked through the living room, until she found the door let open especially for her.

- ''Hmm… all this space, ground, and grass and trees, this is mine! I wonder what are they doing? What is that tall thing over there, or this alley, where does it takes to?''

And without giving any thoughts, she starts taking a few rounds, in all directions, climbing on a tree, playing with a leaf, tumbling down, and with speed, disappears in the back of the yard.

Not long after, going with some water for the flowers, we were amused to find her, waiting at the corner of the house, as if she was hunting , and when she got eye to eye with us, with the speed of a feline, she runes by us and continues to run until we lost track on her.

That day she run through the yard with such a joy, that wormed our hearts and make us very happy about the decision of having a kitty. It is an emotion that we have never felt before, of thrilling joy, and constant amaze.

What an adorable creature!

In the night, she comes in the house to eat, does her spa ritual, and afterwards finds a cozy place, between us, on the couch and falls asleep like she had run the entire world in one day.

5 THE STORY ABOUT DAILY RUTINE

Kitty life! Living in her own term, always finding something interesting to do to entertain herself, always on the run, and always relaxing this kitty looks like she has the entire world just for her. I believe she knows it too.

Each day with her in our home is a constant wonder, of things she does, how she seems to have a very full, yet organized schedule, well planned and diverse in the same time life.

In the night she chooses her place to sleep, of course dictated by comfort, and closeness, she often comes in bed after we are already tucked in, and just slowly sleeps without making a sound near one of us.

Sometimes she stays there all night, other times she moves, on the bed area or even goes to her place.

She does as she pleases!

Then in the morning she usually takes a run through the yard, and as we put the breakfast in her plate, she comes running, starving from all this outdoor morning exercise.

After drinking her water, in a matter of minutes, starts the spa session, when she takes care to look like a cutie for the rest of the day.

No beauty effort stays unrewarded with a beauty sleep, on the couch, in the bed, on the terrace, or even in the yard this is a moment that she never fails to have, but she always chooses carefully to be cozy, near someone or at least with the sun on her face.

Even having new playmate, the beauty sleep must be respected, and without realizing, sometimes she falls asleep while playing.

Peaceful unbothered sleep, how else to be so beautiful?!

Play & Sleep!

6 THE STORY ABOUT KITTY NAME

From the beginning we said that we would not choose a name for her, that we will let her show us things that are characteristic for her, and this is how she will pick her own name.

And yes, for a while we didn't call her any name just sweet kitty.

Playing many times with her I noticed that she is extremely agile and had an amazing speed at grabbing my hand.

I was playing ahead and talked with her, about how cute she is, how fast she moves, and how she has this amazing reddish puffy fur.

After buffering a few seconds on the possible outcomes from this aspect's association, I just told her:

- Hey you are Chili Pepper.

And she stopped for a second from eating my hand, and seemed to be ok with that, and continued playing and rolling in my arms.

As simple as that, this sweet kitty, was the feline metaphor of a sweet red-hot chili pepper, with all her feistiness, and her reddish puffy fur, and sweet eyes.

From that moment on we called her Chili

Pepper and as if she was pleased with the fact that we finally found the name she had, she was and still is always coming when we call her.

And as great findings are exhausting, she fell asleep on the couch, on that soft sweater that now she looks by herself for many afternoon naps.

Sweet Chili Pepper

7 THE STORY ABOUT "BLEND IN"

The only time are hearing her is when she wants to go out in the yard. She eider comes where we are and says "miauu" and then lead us to the door or just stays in front of the door as if she is telling us:

- "I want out!" and if it takes us a while to notice her, she is saying a short "miau" as if she is trying to say. – "Please, I am here at the door, you know I want out!"

She has her cute ways of telling us what she wants, for example food. When she wants food, she goes to her plate, and if she has it, she just slowly starts to eat and then cleans herself, and sleeps, we don't even know she is there.

But if she is out of food in her plate, this is another story, she comes in a hurry she" miaus" once and then in the same hurry she lives, and waits near her plate.

And after a good meal, what comes next?!

Of course, a nice spa session and a good beauty sleep, and depending on the mood she picks whatever place she likes.

- "Hmm…that is strange, she's missing

for a while, but nobody opened the door, and she didn't ask herself out!"

Right under out nose, extremely chilled and relaxed she is sleeping as if this is exactly what she had to do now, not knowing and not caring that, for the past 20 minutes we were wondering where can she be?!

8 THE STORY "COZY" IS MY MIDDLE NAME

It was one of that autumn rainy days, when only looking outside, gives you chills. After a nice breakfast with coffee company and playful morning, Chili accompanied me in the kitchen, to prepare something for lunch.

From the start she approved the idea of anything I do, as long is with meat, and after few sample testing's, she left, this meaning that she gives me her ok.

After I got her approval I continue with the rest of preparations, and I must say that she trusts me in doing it all the way, because from that moment on she left me in charge of the kitchen.

We have a great relationship, and we understand very well each other, I let her space to stay all over the house, wherever she wants, and she lets me in the kitchen, of course after first, giving me her approval.

As I am standing at the kitchen table and enjoying my relaxation moment, I see Chili, across the living sleeping like a round puffy ball near one of her nap bodies.

I know how soft and cozy is that bear, it was mine before Chili took it.

And to see Chili Pepper looking for his coziness makes me smile, as if she knows exactly that sleeping there, is the best thing to do in a rainy day.

9 THE STORY ABOUT THE BIRTHDAY PRESENT

From all the places we found her, this one is special for me.

In the morning we had our coffee on the terrace, enjoying the soft touch of sun. It is day by day nicer to stay outside and enjoy nature, and this is a pleasure for Chili too, running and hiding all day in the yard, laying down in the sun and playing with our shoes, or other things in the yard, because she always finds something to play with nonmatter where she is.

She has her rituals, and activities.

This is one of those days when after staying with us in the morning, she runs of in the yard to play and we wouldn't see her until the afternoon, when all of a sudden climbing on the kitchen window she is "miauing", sign that she is very hungry.

After half a day of enjoying freedom all over the place, ours and the neighbors, she was extremely vocal and anxious to make me understand that she wants food!

I barely managed to put something in her plate, that excited she is. She starts to eat as if she is enjoying and defending her food in the same time.

Why one of my favorite moments?!

Well, after she eat like a spartan, and did her spa moment on the terrace, I have found her under the flowers I received that day, looking at me with her cute face, like she is saying:

- "Happy birthday! I thought all day how to surprise you!"

Surprise!!!

10 THE STORY ABOUT BEST BUDS

We all have or heard about people, that when put their head on the pillow, that's it, they fall asleep almost instantly.

No matter if you are speaking or even if he is speaking, when he reaches the pillow, the sleep it's on. Good night, day, nap all types of sleep. I know this well!

With a smiley face, I try to be nice and say:

- "Lie down, you fall asleep"
And, in a matter of second the sleep is on again.

This time is amazing to see, how this relaxing day nap becomes funniest than ever, because instead of seeing a sleepy man, now I see a sleepy man and a sleepy cat, best buddies being sleeping pills one for the other.

This are precious moments that Chili Pepper, is constantly sharing with us!!!

Sweet kitty Chili Pepper

We love you Peppy!

ABOUT THE AUTHOR

With Chili Pepper I managed to discover things about myself that I never knew, or felt. She is a natural cute, full of affection. Is that unexpected someone that changed our life's.

I can now say without a doubt, that Chili Pepper is the best thing that happened to our family. We are blessed to have this experience in our life.

I hope you all enjoy these stories and don't forget life is surprising, enjoy it!

C.P. Espien